EMMANUEL JOSEPH

From Podium to Progress, How Public Speaking Fuels Leadership and Innovation

Copyright © 2025 by Emmanuel Joseph

All rights reserved. No part of this publication may be reproduced, stored or transmitted in any form or by any means, electronic, mechanical, photocopying, recording, scanning, or otherwise without written permission from the publisher. It is illegal to copy this book, post it to a website, or distribute it by any other means without permission.

First edition

This book was professionally typeset on Reedsy.
Find out more at reedsy.com

Contents

1	Chapter 1: The Power of Public Speaking	1
2	Chapter 2: Overcoming the Fear of Public Speaking	3
3	Chapter 3: Crafting a Compelling Message	5
4	Chapter 4: Engaging the Audience	7
5	Chapter 5: Building Confidence through Practice	9
6	Chapter 6: The Role of Body Language	11
7	Chapter 11: Handling Q&A Sessions	16
8	Chapter 12: The Importance of Feedback	18
9	Chapter 13: The Role of Public Speaking in Innovation	20
10	Chapter 14: Public Speaking and Leadership Development	22
11	Chapter 15: The Role of Public Speaking in Crisis Management	24
12	Chapter 16: Leveraging Public Speaking for Advocacy	26
13	Chapter 17: The Future of Public Speaking	28

1

Chapter 1: The Power of Public Speaking

Public speaking is more than just a skill; it's a transformative tool that can propel leaders to new heights. Effective communicators captivate audiences, inspiring them to take action and embrace change. When a leader speaks with conviction and clarity, they can unify teams, foster collaboration, and drive organizational success. Public speaking also provides a platform for leaders to share their vision, values, and goals, creating a sense of purpose and direction for their followers.

In addition to inspiring others, public speaking allows leaders to establish their credibility and authority. By articulating their expertise and insights, leaders can gain the trust and respect of their audience. This trust is crucial for building strong relationships and influencing others to support their initiatives. Furthermore, public speaking enables leaders to address challenges and opportunities head-on, demonstrating their resilience and adaptability.

Public speaking also plays a critical role in personal development. As leaders hone their speaking skills, they become more self-aware and confident. This self-assurance translates into other areas of their lives, empowering them to tackle complex problems and make bold decisions. Moreover, public speaking fosters a growth mindset, encouraging leaders to continuously seek improvement and embrace new learning experiences.

Ultimately, the power of public speaking lies in its ability to create meaningful connections. By engaging with their audience on an emotional level, leaders can foster empathy and understanding. This emotional resonance not only strengthens relationships but also drives collective action, paving the way for progress and innovation.

2

Chapter 2: Overcoming the Fear of Public Speaking

Fear of public speaking is a common challenge that many leaders face. This fear can be paralyzing, preventing individuals from effectively communicating their ideas and vision. However, overcoming this fear is essential for personal and professional growth. By addressing the root causes of this anxiety, leaders can develop strategies to conquer their apprehension and become more effective communicators.

One of the primary reasons for the fear of public speaking is the fear of judgment. Leaders may worry about how they will be perceived by their audience and whether they will meet their expectations. To overcome this fear, it is important to shift the focus from oneself to the audience. By concentrating on delivering value and addressing the needs and interests of the audience, leaders can alleviate some of the pressure and anxiety associated with public speaking.

Another common cause of public speaking anxiety is the fear of failure. Leaders may be concerned about making mistakes or forgetting their lines. To mitigate this fear, thorough preparation and practice are crucial. By familiarizing themselves with their content and rehearsing their speech multiple times, leaders can build confidence and reduce the likelihood of errors. Additionally, embracing a mindset that views mistakes as learning opportunities can help leaders develop resilience and adaptability.

Physical symptoms of anxiety, such as increased heart rate and sweating, can also exacerbate the fear of public speaking. To manage these physiological responses, leaders can incorporate relaxation techniques into their preparation routine. Deep breathing exercises, visualization, and positive affirmations can help calm nerves and promote a sense of calmness and control.

Ultimately, overcoming the fear of public speaking requires a commitment to continuous improvement and self-reflection. By seeking feedback from others, leaders can identify areas for growth and refine their speaking skills. This iterative process not only helps build confidence but also fosters a growth mindset, enabling leaders to embrace new challenges and opportunities.

3

Chapter 3: Crafting a Compelling Message

A compelling message is the cornerstone of effective public speaking. It is the vehicle through which leaders convey their ideas, vision, and goals to their audience. To craft a powerful message, leaders must first identify the core purpose of their speech. This purpose should align with the needs and interests of the audience and address a specific problem or opportunity.

Once the purpose is established, leaders can begin to develop the content of their message. A well-structured message typically consists of three main components: an introduction, a body, and a conclusion. The introduction should capture the audience's attention and provide a clear overview of the topic. This can be achieved through a compelling anecdote, a surprising statistic, or a thought-provoking question.

The body of the message should present the main points and supporting evidence in a logical and organized manner. Each point should be clearly articulated and backed by relevant data, examples, or stories. It is important to maintain a balance between providing enough detail to inform the audience and keeping the content concise and focused. Transitions between points should be smooth and seamless, guiding the audience through the narrative.

The conclusion of the message should reinforce the key takeaways and leave a lasting impression on the audience. This can be achieved by summarizing the main points, reiterating the core purpose, and ending with a powerful call to action. The conclusion should also provide a sense of closure and resolution, leaving the audience feeling satisfied and inspired.

In addition to the structure and content, the delivery of the message plays a crucial role in its impact. Leaders should use a confident and engaging tone, varying their pitch and pace to maintain the audience's interest. Non-verbal cues, such as eye contact, gestures, and facial expressions, can also enhance the delivery and reinforce the message. By crafting and delivering a compelling message, leaders can effectively communicate their vision and inspire action.

4

Chapter 4: Engaging the Audience

Engaging the audience is a vital aspect of public speaking that can significantly enhance the impact of a speech. When leaders connect with their audience, they can foster a sense of rapport and trust, making their message more persuasive and memorable. There are several strategies that leaders can employ to create an engaging and interactive experience for their audience.

One effective way to engage the audience is through storytelling. Stories have the power to evoke emotions, create relatable experiences, and simplify complex concepts. By sharing personal anecdotes, case studies, or hypothetical scenarios, leaders can make their message more relatable and compelling. Additionally, incorporating elements of drama, humor, and suspense can captivate the audience's attention and keep them engaged throughout the speech.

Another strategy for engaging the audience is to involve them in the conversation. This can be achieved through interactive techniques such as asking questions, conducting polls, or encouraging audience participation. By inviting the audience to share their thoughts and experiences, leaders can create a sense of involvement and ownership, making the speech more dynamic and memorable. Additionally, responding to audience feedback and adapting the speech accordingly can demonstrate empathy and flexibility, further strengthening the connection with the audience.

Visual aids, such as slides, videos, and props, can also enhance audience engagement by providing a visual representation of the key points. Visual aids can help clarify complex information, reinforce the message, and maintain the audience's interest. However, it is important to use visual aids judiciously and ensure that they complement, rather than overshadow, the spoken content.

Finally, effective use of body language can significantly enhance audience engagement. Leaders should maintain eye contact with the audience, use open and expressive gestures, and move confidently on stage. These non-verbal cues can convey enthusiasm, credibility, and approachability, making the audience more receptive to the message. By employing these strategies, leaders can create an engaging and impactful public speaking experience.

5

Chapter 5: Building Confidence through Practice

Confidence is a critical component of successful public speaking. When leaders exude confidence, they can command the attention and respect of their audience, making their message more persuasive and impactful. Building confidence in public speaking requires consistent practice and a commitment to continuous improvement.

One of the most effective ways to build confidence is through regular practice and rehearsal. Leaders should familiarize themselves with their content and practice delivering their speech multiple times. This can help them internalize the key points, improve their delivery, and reduce the likelihood of errors. Additionally, practicing in front of a mirror or recording the speech can provide valuable feedback and help leaders identify areas for improvement.

Another important aspect of building confidence is developing a positive mindset. Leaders should focus on their strengths and accomplishments, and visualize themselves delivering a successful speech. Positive affirmations and self-encouragement can also help boost self-esteem and reduce anxiety. It is important to remember that confidence is built over time, and each speaking opportunity is a chance to learn and grow.

Seeking feedback from others is another valuable strategy for building confidence. Constructive feedback from trusted colleagues, mentors, or coaches can provide insights into areas for improvement and help leaders refine their speaking skills. It is important to approach feedback with an open mind and a willingness to learn, as this can lead to continuous growth and development.

Finally, building confidence requires a willingness to step outside of one's comfort zone. Leaders should seek out opportunities to speak in front of different audiences and in various settings. This can help them develop resilience and adaptability, and build confidence in their ability to handle diverse speaking situations. By consistently challenging themselves and embracing new opportunities, leaders can build the confidence needed to excel in public speaking.

6

Chapter 6: The Role of Body Language

Body language is a powerful tool that can significantly enhance the impact of a speech. Non-verbal cues, such as gestures, facial expressions, and posture, can convey emotions, reinforce the message, and create a connection with the audience. Understanding and effectively using body language is essential for successful public speaking.

One of the key elements of body language is eye contact. Maintaining eye contact with the audience can create a sense of connection and engagement, making the audience feel valued and involved. Leaders should strive to make eye contact with different members of the audience, rather than focusing on a single point. This can help create a sense of inclusivity and rapport.

Gestures are another important aspect of body language. Effective use of gestures can emphasize key points, illustrate concepts, and add energy to the speech. Leaders should use open and expressive gestures, avoiding repetitive or distracting movements. It is important to ensure that gestures are natural and complement the spoken content, rather than overshadowing it.

Facial expressions also play a crucial role in conveying emotions and reinforcing the message. Leaders should use appropriate facial expressions to convey enthusiasm, empathy, and confidence. Smiling, for example, can create a warm and approachable demeanor, while a serious expression can emphasize the gravity of a particular point. By being mindful of their facial expressions, leaders can enhance their connection with the audience and make their message more impactful.

Posture is another key aspect of body language. Leaders should maintain an upright and open posture, as this conveys confidence and authority. Avoiding slouching or closed-off positions, such as crossing arms, is important for projecting a positive and engaging presence. Additionally, moving purposefully on stage can add energy to the speech and help maintain the audience's attention.

By understanding and effectively using body language, leaders can enhance their public speaking skills and create a more engaging and persuasive experience for their audience.

Chapter 7: Mastering the Art of Persuasion Persuasion is a fundamental aspect of public speaking that can influence opinions, drive action, and inspire change. To master the art of persuasion, leaders must understand the principles of effective persuasion and apply them in their speeches.

One key principle of persuasion is establishing credibility. Leaders can build credibility by demonstrating their expertise, sharing relevant experiences, and providing evidence to support their claims. Credibility is also enhanced through consistency and integrity, as leaders who consistently deliver on their promises and uphold their values are more likely to gain the trust of their audience.

Another principle of persuasion is appealing to emotions. Emotions have a powerful impact on decision-making, and leaders who can evoke emotions such as empathy, excitement, or urgency can create a stronger connection with their audience. Using storytelling, vivid imagery, and personal anecdotes can help elicit emotional responses and make the message more memorable.

Logical reasoning is also a critical component of persuasion. Leaders should present clear and rational arguments, supported by evidence and data. Organizing the content in a logical and coherent manner helps the audience follow the argument and understand the key points. Additionally, addressing potential counterarguments and providing rebuttals can strengthen the persuasiveness of the message.

By mastering the art of persuasion, leaders can effectively influence their audience and drive meaningful change.

Chapter 8: Utilizing Visual Aids Visual aids are powerful tools that can enhance the impact of a speech by providing visual representation of key points and concepts. When used effectively, visual aids can help clarify complex information, reinforce the message, and maintain the audience's interest.

One of the most common types of visual aids is slides. Slides can be used to present text, images, graphs, and videos, providing a visual supplement to the spoken content. When creating slides, it is important to keep them simple and uncluttered, focusing on key points rather than overwhelming the audience with too much information. Using high-quality images and graphics can also enhance the visual appeal of the slides and make the content more engaging.

Another type of visual aid is props. Props can be used to illustrate a point, demonstrate a concept, or add a tangible element to the speech. For example, a leader discussing a new product might use a prototype or sample to provide a hands-on demonstration. Props should be relevant to the content and used sparingly to avoid distraction.

Videos can also be effective visual aids, providing dynamic and engaging content that can reinforce the message. Videos can be used to share testimonials, showcase case studies, or provide visual examples of key points. When using videos, it is important to ensure they are high-quality, relevant to the content, and appropriately timed within the speech.

By utilizing visual aids effectively, leaders can enhance their public speaking skills and create a more engaging and impactful experience for their audience.

Chapter 9: Connecting with Diverse Audiences Public speaking often involves addressing diverse audiences with varying backgrounds, interests, and perspectives. To connect with diverse audiences, leaders must be culturally sensitive, inclusive, and adaptable in their approach.

One important aspect of connecting with diverse audiences is understanding their needs and interests. Leaders should research their audience and tailor their content to address relevant issues and concerns. This can involve using examples and references that resonate with the audience, as well as acknowledging and respecting their cultural values and norms.

Inclusivity is also key to connecting with diverse audiences. Leaders should use inclusive language and avoid stereotypes or assumptions. Making an effort to pronounce names correctly and recognize diverse perspectives can create a sense of respect and appreciation. Additionally, providing opportunities for audience participation and feedback can foster a sense of involvement and ownership.

Adaptability is crucial when addressing diverse audiences. Leaders should be prepared to adjust their content and delivery based on the audience's reactions and feedback. This can involve modifying the language, tone, or pacing to better align with the audience's preferences and expectations. Being open to feedback and willing to make changes can demonstrate empathy and flexibility.

By connecting with diverse audiences, leaders can create a more inclusive and engaging public speaking experience, fostering understanding and collaboration.

Chapter 10: The Impact of Storytelling Storytelling is a powerful tool that can transform a speech and make it more memorable and impactful. Stories have the ability to evoke emotions, create relatable experiences, and simplify complex concepts. By incorporating storytelling into their speeches, leaders can enhance their communication and connect more deeply with their audience.

One of the key elements of effective storytelling is authenticity. Leaders should share personal stories and experiences that are genuine and relevant to the message. Authentic stories can create a sense of relatability and trust, making the audience more receptive to the message.

Another important aspect of storytelling is structure. A well-structured story typically follows a narrative arc, consisting of a beginning, middle, and end. The beginning should introduce the characters and setting, while the middle presents the main conflict or challenge. The end should provide a resolution and convey the key takeaway. By following this structure, leaders can create a compelling and cohesive narrative that engages the audience.

Using vivid imagery and descriptive language can also enhance the impact of storytelling. By painting a clear picture in the audience's mind, leaders can make the story more vivid and memorable. Additionally, incorporating dialogue and sensory details can add depth and richness to the narrative.

By mastering the art of storytelling, leaders can create a more engaging and impactful public speaking experience, inspiring and motivating their audience.

7

Chapter 11: Handling Q&A Sessions

Q&A sessions can be an integral part of public speaking, providing an opportunity for the audience to engage with the speaker and seek clarification on key points. Effectively handling Q&A sessions requires preparation, active listening, and the ability to think on one's feet.

Preparation is key to handling Q&A sessions with confidence. Leaders should anticipate potential questions and prepare responses in advance. This involves understanding the key points of the speech, identifying areas where the audience may seek further information, and considering possible counterarguments. By being well-prepared, leaders can respond to questions more effectively and confidently.

Active listening is crucial during Q&A sessions. Leaders should listen carefully to each question, ensuring they fully understand it before responding. This involves maintaining eye contact, nodding, and providing verbal affirmations to show engagement. If a question is unclear, leaders should ask for clarification before providing a response. Active listening not only helps provide accurate answers but also demonstrates respect and attentiveness to the audience.

When responding to questions, leaders should be concise and focused. They should address the specific question and avoid going off on tangents. If they do not know the answer to a question, it is important to be honest and offer to follow up with the information later. This demonstrates integrity

CHAPTER 11: HANDLING Q&A SESSIONS

and a commitment to providing accurate information.

By effectively handling Q&A sessions, leaders can foster a sense of engagement and trust, creating a more interactive and valuable public speaking experience.

8

Chapter 12: The Importance of Feedback

Feedback is a valuable tool for improving public speaking skills and achieving continuous growth. Constructive feedback provides insights into strengths and areas for improvement, helping leaders refine their content and delivery.

Seeking feedback from a variety of sources, such as colleagues, mentors, and audience members, can provide diverse perspectives and a more comprehensive understanding of one's performance. Leaders should approach feedback with an open mind and a willingness to learn, viewing it as an opportunity for growth rather than criticism.

When receiving feedback, it is important to listen actively and ask for specific examples and suggestions for improvement. This can help leaders understand the feedback more clearly and identify actionable steps for enhancement. Leaders should also take time to reflect on the feedback and consider how it aligns with their goals and values.

Providing feedback to others is also an important aspect of personal and professional development. By offering constructive feedback to peers and colleagues, leaders can contribute to their growth and create a culture of continuous improvement. Providing feedback in a respectful and supportive manner, focusing on specific behaviors and offering actionable suggestions, can help build positive relationships and foster a growth mindset.

By valuing and embracing feedback, leaders can continuously enhance their

CHAPTER 12: THE IMPORTANCE OF FEEDBACK

public speaking skills and achieve greater success in their communication efforts.

9

Chapter 13: The Role of Public Speaking in Innovation

Public speaking plays a significant role in driving innovation and fostering a culture of creativity. By effectively communicating ideas and inspiring others, leaders can create an environment that encourages innovation and collaboration.

One way public speaking contributes to innovation is by sharing new ideas and perspectives. Leaders who articulate their vision and share innovative concepts can inspire others to think creatively and explore new possibilities. This can lead to the generation of new ideas and the development of innovative solutions to challenges.

Public speaking also facilitates collaboration and knowledge sharing. By engaging with diverse audiences and encouraging open dialogue, leaders can create a platform for the exchange of ideas and insights. This collaborative approach can lead to the discovery of new opportunities and the development of innovative strategies.

Additionally, public speaking can help create a culture of experimentation and risk-taking. Leaders who communicate a vision of innovation and emphasize the importance of learning from failure can encourage others to take bold steps and explore new approaches. This can foster a mindset of continuous improvement and drive the organization toward greater

CHAPTER 13: THE ROLE OF PUBLIC SPEAKING IN INNOVATION

innovation.

By leveraging the power of public speaking, leaders can create a culture of innovation that drives progress and success.

10

Chapter 14: Public Speaking and Leadership Development

Public speaking is a critical component of leadership development, as it enhances key skills and attributes necessary for effective leadership. By honing their public speaking abilities, leaders can strengthen their communication, influence, and decision-making skills.

Effective communication is a cornerstone of leadership, and public speaking provides a platform for leaders to articulate their vision, values, and goals. By delivering clear and compelling messages, leaders can inspire and motivate their teams, fostering a sense of purpose and direction.

Public speaking also enhances leaders' ability to influence others. By mastering the art of persuasion and storytelling, leaders can effectively convey their ideas and gain buy-in from stakeholders. This ability to influence is crucial for driving change and achieving organizational objectives.

Decision-making is another key aspect of leadership that can be enhanced through public speaking. By presenting information and arguments in a structured and logical manner, leaders can improve their critical thinking and analytical skills. This can lead to more informed and effective decision-making.

Furthermore, public speaking fosters self-awareness and confidence, as leaders gain feedback and reflect on their performance. This self-awareness can lead to personal growth and development, helping leaders become more effective and impactful.

By incorporating public speaking into their leadership development, leaders can enhance their skills and achieve greater success in their roles.

11

Chapter 15: The Role of Public Speaking in Crisis Management

In times of crisis, effective communication is crucial for guiding teams, reassuring stakeholders, and maintaining stability. Public speaking plays a vital role in crisis management, as it allows leaders to convey critical information, provide updates, and address concerns.

One key aspect of public speaking in crisis management is transparency. Leaders should communicate openly and honestly about the situation, providing accurate and timely information. Transparency helps build trust and credibility, as stakeholders appreciate leaders who are forthright and accountable. Additionally, being transparent about the challenges and uncertainties can help manage expectations and reduce anxiety.

Another important element is empathy. During a crisis, people may experience fear, stress, and uncertainty. Leaders who acknowledge these emotions and demonstrate empathy can create a sense of understanding and support. Using compassionate language and expressing genuine concern can help foster a sense of solidarity and resilience.

Clarity is also essential in crisis communication. Leaders should provide clear and concise messages, avoiding jargon or ambiguous language. This helps ensure that the audience understands the key points and knows what actions to take. Additionally, providing regular updates and maintaining open

CHAPTER 15: THE ROLE OF PUBLIC SPEAKING IN CRISIS MANAGEMENT

lines of communication can help keep stakeholders informed and engaged.

By effectively using public speaking in crisis management, leaders can guide their teams through challenging times and foster a sense of stability and resilience.

12

Chapter 16: Leveraging Public Speaking for Advocacy

Public speaking is a powerful tool for advocacy, allowing leaders to raise awareness, mobilize support, and drive social change. By effectively communicating their message, leaders can influence public opinion, shape policy, and inspire collective action.

One of the key elements of advocacy through public speaking is passion. Leaders who speak with passion and conviction can capture the audience's attention and inspire them to take action. Sharing personal stories and experiences can help convey the urgency and importance of the cause, making it more relatable and compelling.

Another important aspect is framing the message. Leaders should frame their message in a way that resonates with the audience and aligns with their values and interests. This involves understanding the audience's perspective and tailoring the content to address their concerns and motivations. Using persuasive language and rhetorical techniques can also enhance the impact of the message.

Building alliances and coalitions is also crucial for effective advocacy. Public speaking provides an opportunity to connect with like-minded individuals and organizations, creating a unified and powerful voice. Collaborating with others and amplifying each other's messages can increase the reach and

CHAPTER 16: LEVERAGING PUBLIC SPEAKING FOR ADVOCACY

impact of the advocacy efforts.

By leveraging public speaking for advocacy, leaders can drive meaningful change and make a positive impact on society.

13

Chapter 17: The Future of Public Speaking

The landscape of public speaking is continually evolving, influenced by technological advancements, changing communication trends, and the dynamic nature of audiences. To stay relevant and effective, leaders must adapt to these changes and embrace new opportunities.

One significant trend shaping the future of public speaking is the rise of digital platforms. Virtual presentations, webinars, and live streaming have become increasingly popular, allowing leaders to reach global audiences and engage with them in real-time. Embracing digital platforms requires leaders to develop new skills, such as mastering virtual presentation tools and creating engaging online content.

Another trend is the growing importance of diversity and inclusion. Audiences today are more diverse than ever, and leaders must be mindful of cultural sensitivities and inclusive practices. This involves using inclusive language, representing diverse perspectives, and creating an environment where everyone feels valued and heard.

The future of public speaking also involves leveraging data and analytics. By analyzing audience feedback and engagement metrics, leaders can gain insights into their performance and identify areas for improvement. This data-driven approach can help leaders refine their content, tailor their messages, and enhance their overall effectiveness.

Innovation in public speaking is also driven by emerging technologies such as artificial intelligence, augmented reality, and virtual reality. These technologies offer new ways to create immersive and interactive experiences, making public speaking more dynamic and engaging.

By staying informed about these trends and embracing new opportunities, leaders can continue to excel in public speaking and drive progress and innovation.

From Podium to Progress: How Public Speaking Fuels Leadership and Innovation explores the transformative power of public speaking in shaping effective leadership and driving innovation. Through seventeen insightful chapters, this book delves into the various aspects of public speaking, providing practical strategies and inspiring examples.

The journey begins by highlighting the significance of public speaking in leadership, emphasizing how effective communicators can inspire, unify, and build credibility. It then addresses common fears associated with public speaking and offers strategies to overcome them. Readers will learn how to craft compelling messages, engage diverse audiences, and use body language to enhance their delivery.

The book also delves into the art of persuasion, the impact of visual aids, and the importance of storytelling. Leaders will discover how to build confidence through practice, handle Q&A sessions with ease, and leverage feedback for continuous improvement. The role of public speaking in crisis management, advocacy, and innovation is thoroughly examined, showcasing how leaders can use their voice to guide, influence, and inspire change.

By the end of the book, readers will have gained valuable insights into the evolving landscape of public speaking and its critical role in leadership development. They will be equipped with the tools and confidence to harness the power of public speaking and drive progress in their organizations and communities.

www.ingramcontent.com/pod-product-compliance
Lightning Source LLC
LaVergne TN
LVHW020740090526
838202LV00057BA/6145